The Hiccups Would Not Stop

Written by Robin Bloksberg   Illustrated by Lisa Adams

Modern Curriculum Press
A Division of Simon & Schuster
299 Jefferson Road, P.O. Box 480
Parsippany, NJ 07054 - 0480

Design and production by BIG BLUE DOT

ISBN: 0-8136-2168-2 Modern Curriculum Press

1 2 3 4 5 6 7 8 9 10 SP 01 00 99 98 97 96 95

Oh, no! Jo had the hiccups.

Hic–hic–hic.

The hiccups would not stop.

She went to her mom.
"Can you–hic–help me make them stop?"

"I hope so," said Mom.
She gave Jo a glass of water.
"Drink it slowly," said Mom.

So Jo drank the water.

But when she stopped,
the hiccups did not.

7

Jo had to make the hiccups stop.

She went to her Aunt Mo.

"Can you–hic–help me make them stop?"

"I hope so," said Aunt Mo.

She gave Jo an ice cream pop.

"Eat this as fast as you can," she said.

So Jo ate the pop,
but the hiccups did not stop.

Jo had to make the hiccups stop.

She went to her friend Bob.

"Can you–hic–help me make them stop?"

"I hope so," said Bob.

He gave Jo a paper bag.

"Blow like this," said Bob.

So Jo blew into the bag.

And what do you know?
Jo's hiccups stopped.

14

"Thank you, Bob," said Jo.
"My hiccups stopped."

"You're–hic–welcome," said Bob.

Oh, no!